TERROR

Terror ©2014 by Bethany Price. Published in the United States by Vegetarian Alcoholic Press. No part of this book may be reproduced in any fashion, save short quotation for the purpose of literary review, without the written consent of the author. For information, contact vegalpress@gmail.com

Cover art: ***Convo between Horse and Chino during Full Moon*** by **Skye**, ink on canvas, 2013

Some of the poems in ***Tarot*** have previously been featured online in **BlazeVOX**.

I. Tarot, or what's inside:

Mother of Blades - Libra, Skadi-the North Wind
  8

Seven of Cups - Jealousy
  9

Six of Cups - Compassion
  10

Shakti - the Life Dancer
  11

Two of Cups - Whirlpool
  12

Eight of Flames - Burnout
  13

Fire of Cups - The Storm
  14

Maiden of Blades - Gemini, Hina
  16

Crone of Flames - Sagittarius, Cerridwen
  17

Three of Pentacles - Aruru, Claywoman
  18

the Witch
  19

Four of Blades - Deception
                                        20

Isis, the Priestess
                                        21

Eight of cups - Withdrawal
                                        22

One of Blades - the Sibyl
                                        23

II. Each Word, or what am I really seeing:

Waiting by your door laughing because I know you aren't home
                                        26

One foot out the faery ring
                                        27

Maybe it will murder, maybe it will breathe
                                        28

Magic is a language for making yourself last
                                        29

III. Renewal, or what will change me:

Rhyme Royal
                                        32

Hungover with a lampshade
                                        34

IV. Recommended for Elsewhere, or disorientation:

   Mistaking Embalming Fluid for Perfume
                                           36

   Odyssea tells her story
                                           39

   Symptoms of alien abduction
                                           43

V. Outlander, or commuting with strangers:

   After Drake's Hold On and Frank Ocean's Pyramids
                                         48

   After the Weeknd
                                           49

   After Welcome to Night Vale
                                         51

   Untitled
                                           52

VI. Restless, or was I right to lose the desire:

   In the woods, we learn
                                         54

Sometimes we fight

58

Lover, I need to love myself

61

Old letters from Dad

62

I. Tarot, or what's inside

(I was born in Oral Roberts' hospital. I've seen people slain in the Holy Spirit. After college I found a tarot deck, Daughters of the Moon, in a used bookstore, hidden among erotica. Time has given me scholastic curiosities of the esoteric and religious, and all the ways we as humans manifest belief in the daunting chaos of the cosmos. Through images that upend our brainwashing we find a refreshing exploration of that which we individually align. Throw off constraints of what you are trained to fear and many pains fall away. Embrace the fear of what you always ignore.)

Mother of Blades - Libra, Skadi - the North Wind

I move as blood in its throat
this beast you'll name
but won't sum up the courage to kill
I wear your belt & follow
the idea   clouding up the air
on a path in deep night

I opened a door in the field
& your comfort followed me in
on all fours   a pet I could
depend on

Every essence is worth its own trouble
I am training you how to love
but I still can't trust properly
in the end
it's a risk
with this ruptured earth

Next time I find your bird
I'll ink it with my lips
hoist it up & hope it comes
back foreign

Seven of Cups - Jealousy

She's undone many mystics
trapped them so long they
became riddled with desire
like bodies after love

How come
no one told me this
(the whole point) if i believe
it   then such it will be

Every cup she touches
spills over
I have a problem
with her boldness
because it fails
every time   I am a reflection
She mirrors me   a new nation
in a hill of eyelids
this is   it is
all the same body

Six of Cups - Compassion

They bless my body
with their hands
they feel
the theatre of it   I wish
her breasts were plates
I could take
answers from   I wish
her braids were snakes
to coil me up
to rise from the shore

Kelpie with tresses like mortar
they build my come back
they offer me food
I am prone   I am weak
with them   I spill out
a body emptied
I am only for me
only for me

Shakti - the Life Dancer

I slipped between time-light
& time-dark   I am wearing
the glass skin of a new
friend   I touch an orange
& scalp an alligator
simultaneously
I have many hands   I let loose
all the names I know   let them
in between
through a strange nude shape

I am an egg baking a meal
with a planet   we make
a separate whole I am
with my mother in law
she laughs at my skillet   I am a skillet
rusted from drunken use
a woman   filled with beer
a star trail   roughly tumbled

Two of Cups - Whirlpool

Can I climb the mountains
can I pierce your ridges
with cloud   I am red
facing grief
completely unmastered
I am loved
by this shore   the sand
& shells completely
at war in me

All else caught
in stillness
exhalations of
the rain

You are a crest
of the sea I can't
reach or taste

Eight of Flames - Burnout

I am a sword's mouth
suckling on your
cliffs   dear fire
I've arrived   your creator

I will travel acres
to avenge
all my mother's houses
I will greet the ultimate
mage   as a friend
uncomplaining

But the ground
will be too hard
the creeping
too far gone

Yesterday my body
breeding heat

Tomorrow weary
with evidential blood
my queendom unpaid for
by my speech   only my hands
know that at the end
I will owe

Fire of Cups - the Storm

I hear it with my teeth
each a piece of neon bait
& the cruel elastic waves
these shapes I make
with my palms
dry heaving dead skin

I was wet with worry
this morning   it broke the land

I demolished stories
any way I could
loved & rushed
into the deep parts
of the world

I'll never know
the obsidian mark
calling its spawn back
fabled with faces
like angler
fish & sea urchins

I chime my toes
a million clocks
& anxious laughs wash
my mouth out

The trees in the yard
long   home-wrecked

& fed
I am a meal for the walls

I run out
settle myself under
the green whipping
crowns

Can I be here forever
can I extend
my own vacancy

Maiden of Blades - Gemini, Hina

I rise up to a sun
lining my limbs   with babble

I emanate silence
I only show my body as braille
to the roaming, the space-torn

My busted shell forms wings
like breasts opened
the ended sky bordering black
occasioned by two planets
covered in marshes
beneath me

I reach new methods
my hands choose
to flake away
the alone-and-old skin

I   in a lost place
couldn't be happier

Crone of Flames - Sagittarius, Cerridwen

Do you talk all the time?
I bet you talk all the time
in your cast iron pot   stirring eons
me   I am yellow
in your hair   a painted sky
lark   I am serious for that hound
the village loves to chase
(your sacrifice forgot to rid of the mountain I made)

I hide in SheWhoKnows I borrowed
a cryptic machine
the same night
this book fell into my hands

Living for the hunt
the dogs are after the salves
in my wrinkles
if I time this in the right way
I'll love through your mouth
and exhale starpig

We are each of us
the hundreds of dots around your night tools
eaves of rock   my cheat sheet
the clicking knobs, the loose
leaves screaming, I open the tome

Your grave
smells like hamhock & vitality

Three of Pentacles, Aruru - Claywoman

You stowed our religion away into a baby
I strapped on my back
put away the broken clay pots
I'd rather take care of us
on premonition alone
    with high peaks
& jagged walks

You've helped me
upend this uncouth skin   the soil we bathe in
devours my fill

But I learn not to be hungry

Will I let the child stretch
as does the cheetah inside me
when she gets old enough I can teach her
how to yarn gold into fulfillment

She will be barefoot
& striped   with my braids
wrapped tight about her
& the tiger teeth of each morning
will bid her to climb

She will paw at my memory
edging around her
a strand of hair she never sees

the Witch

Little french horn of a unicorn
behind the condescending cat
& that hair
full of the rarest thorns

Dagger and flame ground
you   earth kept   I am inept
at reading out loud
these spells I tend
to whisper when power
knocks on the mind

As if   but especially how
do I grow from the ground
& eat the stones you
feed to me   in between the passages
& right after the trees burst
through overnight

The babies are babies
they watched the creatures jump
around the seeds the owl the cat
your body the steam of us all
carefully secret

Moon doomed night

Four of Blades - Deception

I am obscene
at parties
in raw nature
blinded

But I stood on a log
sloughed off my hair
in a crop top
watched a single death
fall in leaf-form
shielded my head
from acorns   stalked a squirrel
as a new water bodied itself
in my ears

Scared and sacred
without a blade

Fondled a clenched
tree   sandals slipping smoothly

Should that sun
give me yonic breathing
I'd relax in the sandy hair
of this meadow-beach

These geographies I cut with
but can't abide

Isis, the Priestess

Mostly planetary
I envisioned you   knowing me
before I knew myself
I searched for some better
godmirror   kept finding
phalluses   repeating
infrastructures

Just like your collar
geometric   pearl heavy
& that egg of the inner
world you hold   eyes
closed   wings crossing
the vial of your strengths
I can't hear yet
but I promise I will keep
listening   if the iota
that I am could break into
the long colorless cloaks of
beyond

My hands stay clumsy
an ancestry
tumbling
my breasted heart healed

Eight of Cups - Withdrawal

Eye drawn to the left
I, night
my moon rises
gathers blood from me in a vial
maybe my feet are firm
& this book chained to me this
cave will let me suck back the poison

But miles away the steam
ascends   the waves troubled
my two shoulders overburdened
hugged with chalk from the gate

You will not see me become old
with meats & fertile dreams
I'm sewn cloth
there should be a gut inside

Yet I've grown dim
please forget about me
for a few months

One of Blades - the Sibyl

Do you sense a pulse
in the tower?

Crystals enlivened me
a marrow engorged with possibility
in your womb-ears I resemble
cliche   still I am to be my own

In my prophecy
your hair was a lake
& I an accidental ceiling
to a haunted land

I was studied by
a peach man in the sky
I was punished

All this soil we have to breathe through
we'll die by the very act
& make it through by fire

To grow
break open
hot

II. Each Word, or what am I really seeing

(Often the supposedly sick of mind will dream and cling to hidden conspiracies, messages in media and cultural patterns. Others stand in sidewalks, blog, or speak to impatient commuters about dangers we are unknowingly facing. The most luminescent room could be your end. The catchiest song will encourage you to rape and maim and degrade the divinity in you. Should we take our time to decode the medium? Our head will hurt from the effort. Each word's beginning could bring you across to a reality I don't have the courage to say.)

Waiting by your door laughing because I know you aren't home

Clairvoyant, eldritch river:
undoubted Logos.
Enemies assign
new metaphors, each
abstracts time. (Ill numbers
remain after inspection,
never falls away.)
Lions languidly yellow
offstage, unresponsive
visions. Enormous nebulas
erotically vacate essence. Rogue
loins onshore, omens
knowingly emoted:
dear usurper, gentle
liar: in evil rollicking,
ordinary roads meet
odious ravens.
Envoys renew Epicurean
philosophy. Rightly
ecstatic, such swelling
eases damnation.

One foot out the faery ring

We envy acknowledged ruffians.
Error pollutes and regal effort designs all.
With acumen, you dwindle ordination.
Wishful nonsense translocates,
or caterwauls offensively.
Relatively eager seeds
yoke over. Uncomfortable rubble.
Collapsed opulence
naturally slants through aching.
Nearby toxins wane. All sexual gains
open doors. Demonic eaves sigh
surreptitiously.
Inside authority, money breeds.
Electronic Rorschachs each follow
the other, falling below.
'Ere lunar interims end, forbear.

Maybe it will murder, maybe it will breathe

Inebriated wildcatter. Aposiopesis lengthens
killing; time hastens evenly.
Ever after, relishing this hell.
Filamentary imagination, nightmare dependent.
Thrills hold aggressive toxins, toward
hearts easily militant. Open
apocalypse, new symbols. Offbeat, five
tremors hiccup inward.
Elevated vitality eats seconds.
Suppose her ample persuasion entails
mangled yokes. Pitfalls each reading
insures. Playtime hermit, erect.
Realms acquire linguistic vibrations.
Iniquities slope into our neighbor's barn.
Estimation: here I need dire
serrations, holistic overflowing wind.
Earlier records call unrest revolutionary,
this almanac is next.
Starry isthmus explains xenomorphic
peril. Every crater tempts touch.
Our fires in need, degenerative mealy
alphas, labias in cellophane.
If our ultimate selfhood subjects
midnight, I lose effective skeletons, witless.
All despair invades nimble giantesses.
Gnashed bellies originate displeasure.
I expect sensory water,
I take hard fright incumbent.
Necromantic salvation.

Magic is a language for making yourself last

Inevitably, dark arts satiate
time - arrested religiously,
deranged lore yields.
We interned towards hate.
Bellowed oval, noxious eardrums,
terrestrial alms sown to eat.
Live in cosmorama, Kraken. Yelp
out. Under clapping is rubbing,
clangorous unmasking.
Loud as rage.
Breaking up twists.
Yonder our uvulas heal ailments,
terrorize each irksome telephone.
Anticipation needs darkness - lifeblood, elements.
A reach needs immortality.
New growth thrills huge innards
so if all make salacious, itch
left. Eliminate negligible trembling.

III. Renewal, or what will change me

(To have a body at all is to be immediately excluded from countless experiences. Through the eye witness accounts, hallucinations, and mythologies of the people before us, we know of incredible beasts and symbology of animal hybrids. Collected in bestiaries we find that turning the pages brings amusement, wonder, or indifference. If we could pop a skin off. If we could gaze through a looking glass and find what will change us, what sort of beast we will become. Tragedy and even routine forge us into strange creatures, but we can't know what it is to break our body away and survive.)

Rhyme Royale

You are such a gorgeous sea-hound;
I mistook you for a sleep-remnant pet
when I woke up. If only I were crowned
in a jewel as crustacean and wet

as you, a water beast breathing the sweat
from my legs. But I fill you lovingly with
what I dream of. You give me the whole myth.

I slide awkward and moon filled
from my bed. My wings make no
sense. I hope you won't let me be killed
for them, by the wanderers slow

but sure to arrive from the plateau
glowing down the street. I've heard
they eat meat only from the furred

or freakish creatures from the dark.
If I was a Yeck[1] I could lift a mountain peak
and give them refuge. In the stark
songs of sublime earth they'd speak

only of my power and the bleak
homes they knew before furrowed earth
harbored their heads. A dark rebirth.

---

[1] Small shapeshifting spirit from the folklore of India.

II.

Your crawl is sloppy and phlegmatic.
You are studying my books with touch
and tongue, tripping over titles, asthmatic,
sincere. If I could move like that, in such

intimate ways. But I clutch
the floor with my feet. My scaly pinions
heighten any effort. This dominion

a nocturnal shape-shift takes
over my limbs, and this mirror
I avoid. Quietly my scalp flakes
off in two neat circles, clearer

than glass in their look, nearer
to sickly coasters than obvious flesh.
A Phooka[2]'s laugh ejects fresh

from my mouth. Low and gruff
as if I've just butchered an explorer.
My raw horns are ridged and slough
off an ashy substance. I spy horror

in your eyes, despite your bestial order,
and you pad away quietly, to
fashion me a remedy. A wild brew.

---

[2] Irish goblin, usually appears as a dog, horse, or bull. Offers unwary travelers a lift then dumps them in the ditch.

Hungover with a lampshade

In a hotel room, I am jolted awake.
No being waits for me in the dark,
nor in the empty bed next to me,
but the color of the air is different.

I notice the walls: I am appalled.
They are covered in peeling hair.

A sound from my throat is cloyed
when no locks brush my shoulders:
I raise a hand to my head,

my scalp is floral.
Wallpaper.
Unoffending and bland.

The floor aches with a lusty flesh breath
and my figure doesn't rise or fall.
It's hard to realize it when I touch
my body, it takes me a few seconds
to process,

as I pick splintered wood
from my belly.

IV. Recommended for elsewhere, or disorientation

(You wake up safe in your bed and the space between the eyes adjusting and your brain gathering the night's closing time is a delicious uncertainty. But was anything sinister? Is anything amiss? Is everything where I left it? On a broader scale, it's mostly arbitrary where these shells reside for a lifetime. If we were given resources would we make the choice to stay or find some other cove for our huddling and our inane activity? And what do we leave behind, in books or houses or backyards, what tiny materials collect grime and attest anonymously to the fact that yes, we were here? We were here.)

Mistaking Embalming Fluid for Perfume
(left margin text found on a bundle of tiny notes)

hail Mary
If I had been
there, I would have cut the
cord for you.*
What did he know?   *to sever the monarch head of
          an old story. I made
          babies with you because I liked
          your curved back.

The Holy Spirit
is Really Pissed
off & is coming* to
        *clad in oak tree to preach & hammer
        my head back into the graveyard.
        near the monument, where my
        friend is buried. I'm worried about
        him despite his being dead.
a church near you.

        *are you sure? can I make her
playing priest   bookmarks to use in shadow play?
She is not playing* i'll tell her she smells like junipers to
        brighten the day.

Dorothy Day.
"fill the souls"   *how can you be so pretty, with that
how can you be smeared book, sighing out of your
a Catholic?*   pelvis. I made scrolls with
        you because I like your running
the Church beneath teeth.
the Church thinks

with love & can
hear it.*

    *can feel it can feel it can you feel it?
    I can't get hungry. my foundation
    perfects but my stomach won't get
    clean won't get pastor clean please
    pastor get me clean.

Don't lose heart -
<u>We were made for
these times.</u>
We've been training to meet
here. We are
the leaders we*

    *are meat eaters we need five liters of
    holy spirit fire to rain rebellion. I am
    kept will you let me free? save my
    sisters and my brothers. I learned to
    read, you take every book away.

have been
waiting for.
We are fully

so visioned &
can signal each
other

You are not without
resources & you are not alone.
There are millions
of boats out there
with you. We have
been in training

for these dark
times. We have
been left for dead.

We have perfected
the act of
resurrection.

No matter how many
times we come
back.
Notre Dame Library.*   *that supernatural wood etched into
My Aunt said   flesh and the browser who never
because you can   made it out, the stacks ate her up
read someday   and now her family tells me she was
you will lead   building volumes of empty shelves
them.   to yawn at her while she dreamt.

Stillborn baby
Bishop.
that's not Catholic.
that's not Bishop.*   *that's not a witch in your bed
                                         parting the red sea of your body
                                         why did you kill it?

laughter is a form
of prayer.*
                                      *I will be on my knees all my life.

Odyssea tells her story

I.

He sidled up next to me,
slyly spoke *hey baby we are both*
oozing into other life forms like death
and maybe angeldom you wanna
get together and melt
into the atmosphere?
And boing! The bartender
banged up from under the bar
and offered me something sweet,
a noisome honey, fermented
chemical love. The men like animals,
the women like animals, we roamed
and roamed each notch on that
stool chain until we found
 a soul to wam and mamp with!
The onomatopoeias soaked me
up and the sighs of the compass-oh's
and southward ummms gave me
answer. Dry me with a land towel!
Whole lands raised and twisted
to wring out the tensions! The sex
meeping along the floor. Computer bits
crumbling out the mouth. They spent
too much time in front of a screen, cause
we know what the internet is for.
A loop towards Gavin who is driving
home after a few don't worry though,

highways! The secret is the clarity
coming from ingesting time poisons. Old
Olaf with an ear like a golf ball,
he sees land for miles, he takes
the ship off the dock after farewelling
the folks at the pub.

II.

The folks at the pub
see land for miles, take
coming and going from ingesting time. Old
homes haunt after a few don't worry though!
We know what the internet is for.
Crumbling out the mouth, the pennies they spent
to wring out the tensions! The sex
answers *dry me with a land towel!*
Up heaves the sighs of the compass-oh's,
the soul to wam and mamp with!
Roam each notch on that ladder.
Chemicals love the men like animals
and offer them something sweet,
and boing! The bartender

got it together and melted
into other life forms like death,
who sidled up next to him.

III.

The ship off the dock after farewelling
Olaf with an ear like a golf ball rolling
down a highway. The secret is the clarity
in a loop towards Gavin who is driving with
too much time in front of a screen, cause
meeping along the floor is only weeping. Computer bits
chewed off whole lands, raised and twisted.
Southward heading *ummms* gave me
the onomatopoeic heebie jeebies. They soaked me
on a stool and chained me until they found
the women like animals. Then we roamed
a noisome honey-fermented path to the liquor,
banged up from under the bar.
Into the atmosphere?
And maybe angeldom, you wanna?
I slyly spoke, *hey baby! we are both.*

Symptoms of alien abduction

<u>You leave us no other choice</u>

being prone to compulsive or addictive behavior (kneading your breasts kneading
your breast needing my rest after)

people who awake in a place other than where they went to sleep (waking up in a bed with my siblings, a movie on the screen, laughter and light)

missing time or lost, especially an hour or more (I nap for two minutes but a whole
movie passes)

<u>What will happen to the machine?</u>

suffering abnormal sensitivity (you offend me all the time)

.' "..' ' ":L

(illegible)

fears of sexual relationships ()) (& 7 777

& LATELY WE BARELY TOUCH

\+

\+

We will caress you like an ocean of pure seaweed.

observing balls of light or flashes of light in the home (sleeping in a friend's house
I forget about the window. surrounded by four walls, two strips of light above
don't make sense. I try to ignore voices, to avoid my ears becoming blinded.)

having persistent or especially vivid dreams (so gullible I tend to lose entire lessons, tigers pattering over waterfalls in the kitchen, the wet wind misting my legs as I shift the sheets)

awakening from sleep with soreness in one's genitals (fucked tremendously)

having dreams of especially prominent eyes (my amethyst has become my third
eye but it leaves at times, stares at me through the copse of limbs outside,
rugged corpses with tears for hair)

hearing strange humming

".", '.'", ' " ".".
. . .   .

(I can't hear any comfort through the fuzz)

V. Outlander, or commuting with strangers

(A buxom noisy box churns down a street and we who do not know one another collect and distribute our limbs. We hate potholes. We drown out the drunk people or eavesdrop. I write to pass the time and to hide my eyes. Alternately friendly and cold, never knowing who to trust, better to keep hands busy making feverish pages, listening to music, or a story.)

After Drake's Hold On and Frank Ocean's Pyramids

I can't get over your mark you good-ass girl you baking-my-mind ass girl. you gave me little collections of feudal tribes what does that book in your ma's room worry about. cause you're a troublesome girl and you will realize it/ it's hard to do you alone. hold onto what you think is the one. my gold ass bag. tatted up. you're the girls you're all the girls. I think your certainly something you're a loop so easy to repair its/it's a kick in the gut around you I can't really find my way out. I'm filled with fidget. hold onto the fire in me. it'll comfort you maybe. I've got like a million eyes on me that can't get over your katamari-forever-level of destruction I'll roll you over if granted the chance. you are the very best one to draw me in I've got my eyes balanced on your shoulder. I've marked the zenith of your song please believe me. hold onto anything, but me. you are a vision please tell me. I know exactly. going home is hard. you're my best. the best stranger. tonight is the swiftest and smartest oh justice set one on the loose and he moved his feet just like the body's language.

After the Weeknd

it's got you fairy twisted and sad like what's real anymore drum it sip it dance it baby I don't worry bout you no more = you dun disappeared beneath what the fuck they brought you into - some evidence for you to see enough lights/ touch your own dawn softly w/o healing in your fingers I erase your bad news. it's no room for it. (woah) it's only on top. this anxiety and those oceans of sugar, the danger only edges closer. like a sickness in the intestines or your ex girlfriend wrapped up in trouble tape watch us rock it out or fill these empty drums with our wrap skirts. I might loan you somebody worth it. nothings codeine enough for it. what do you need with all these lights on? do you know what I can finish with your nervous eyes forging thoughts after my crumpled clothes. what it's like to stare at yourself so gone. you got problems w/ my speech? and all the best blue-hatted flight footed kids on your trail. your fade mythologized enough to defend you from abductions. you pour water on time into my ears my skin saves me much danger come at me nature I got bones and muscles for you keep writing about your bitches I'll pass your rivers I got you forever nauseous I only want you to mess up. I can remain blameless and pretty like this track you deceived me with. I hope I'm not w/ it like you think. a paper bag left behind a man's begging. your event is definitely monstrous times two. the yelling. all the money I use to pay for my father's sins, all of em. they say the grays are enemies. be smart and disengage and leave the well alone don't fall down be dangerous be tempting drink deep from yourself all of em can kiss it for you. I want heaven so soon. I have heaved you out from woahdom. give me your girlfriend's sunglasses. gift me your age. we walk around at night in groups. I am defensive because of you. i am through you and onto what's beyond you. i am counting your change I am limp with research we can't make our brains at each other tonight. i am close shaved.

After Welcome to Night Vale

the clockless man knew it was noon. I'm totally not sure about your broadcast. I will never understand your glow cloud. we will move on from life. your face trembles before I fall asleep. this wind is killer music I would like to light you with. or to poke you awake at night. I give away most of what i create. I tell you a lot of spectacles. I can't make my own food I'm a baby. through the frosted glass my veins are just waiting to fail. I create very many dark boxes. a boat called painstaking passes in the water. I need a sign that says "dont approach me". I could write you a black helicopter story just kidding I'm not sure how to tell you terrible things. can i tell you about the barber. will you talk to me soon.

Untitled

flesh touches a mammal lip. recourse on couches so we sleep in past jobs steaming in engines. on the road we puff chested. a boy liked to trip in diamonds but my first impulse was to be petty and hide on public routes avoiding text backs. taking care of a baby with no face. if it was right I wrecked it if my cheeks were mounds I regretted. the anger we thwarted. big thick girls with loose yellow hair.

VI. Restless, or was I right to lose the desire

(Our forms coagulate and deconstruct time in measures of resentment and tenderness. We ask for forgiveness. We flee the scene to be protected. We are alone and tell ourselves differently with lust-bound constructs. We fear a future falling apart and we fear how fiercely we hold our partners to what they should be. How tightly we can suffocate another.)

In the woods, we learn

You wear a weekend ring.

Also, a trench coat. I am heading to a divorce.

And if this isn't enough then
enough isn't this: if me and you,
of course and most certainly eternal.
That's what these letters tell,
huddled, folded over time
in effort and toiled sickness.
The love laying in the bed
when it was barren and then
your womb when it
was filled five times over.

If you want to go inside the cabin, understand most people die that way.

Around this table, I stand like people do when they are false.

Every proclamation I push.
The maze of this highly stubborn,
fretful center won't accomplish much.
When I am around you
I feel nostalgic for places with
mystery, but not for an Atlantis itself,
because my brain reaches
new images and never
heartens to facts.

Leaves of grass cut my feet.

They were your claws burrowing past the planet.

It's not until hours later I register your face pulled
like a nest over the skull.

The Thing that ate them all.
But the two survivors
in the end, drinking and laughing.

*If you saw what I wanted you to, you would laugh till
you cried and you would cry at everything.*

I get stuck.

The paganism in my bed five times,
nostalgic for time's claws.
I had burrowed past your guards
to nest here. Heard it
was dangerous. Delirium
pet me, my skin spilling into
crinkled pages.
Looked in the mirror, found
many futures. No thing
resembles the foliage
of your hair. I smooth it all
down, doubt the depth
of your pornographic intent.
I see now the value,
those animations and new

facts heartening your nerves.

I ate them.

If you want to go inside the cabin, put me in the bed all night. You inherited Atlantis.

I apologize.

I get stuck.

Used through effort, love toils
violently in the shoulders.
It's winter lately, where
I scrunch up to warm up
and end drenched with fatigue.
But I'll pace like a human
is supposed to in the meanest
times. I am cruel,
trying to stand in a road
where I know I'll forget
the spirit inside you.
I control. I am the center.
Bulking myself up for
such a dramatic hibernation.

I will burrow past your guards.

I will wear a coat, refuse to drink with you in your new home.

My face is an obelisk

you can't read because
the features keep blurring.
I pull so much
because I can't feed me
from my own well.

I want to go inside the cabin.

So, usually it's this way that I die.

sometimes we fight

we could have gotten out of bed but we lingered

 and watched the robins
lead discussions of the day.   o b n o x i o u s &
jealous
in their gossip.   but we, too, are birds.   we wrinkled
the bed with our frank nature.   we grew jealous
& watched the leaves   jumping.
 & frailty was there.

& now you are scared somewhere
in the world of this city & I can do nothing but prattle, fidget.

 listen, reader: I want to move   her hair beyond
her shoulder   discover
the properties   of physics   w/ storms inside: I want
to be this pristine complexion, reach   for her pleasure
 across the leaping   bay of concrete,

 halt the moment   in amber muscle. oh girl
among the vintage coats, books, fluorescent lights & scents
of the underworld,   oh fragmented & ugly lily
rent with thunder   through the unkind valley.
only with frailty & movement   are we healed,

only with the beds   of our cities   do we wreck t h e fitted
sheets   of a mind: only with amber, with muscle,
uncouth fragments, this desperate intent   i n names.

each scent in your valley   hid by a t e r r i b l e unmaking,
but I thought I could discover the jumping terrors

of your life   moving beyond nature.   instead I tamed the body
inside your body.   I know you are a Russian doll
I've seen you with speed   put yourself back together
 when I come through the door.

 but baby let's sleep   in the ugly.   if we have no other
means, we will glue ourselves   to the spines of healing books,
sincerely moan as you   the lover   discover my volumes
for what could be our first time.
 there's a wind inside me.

you have fit my muscles with robin eggs. the blue is obnoxious
in the aching light. your mouth on the new city sidewalks

chants your selves back inside.   I   a m
sorry
for prattling,   but I can do nothing but fidget
 around your absent hands in the bed.

Lover, I need to love myself

You fear water but fill yourself up with ocean.

You didn't know what state you were in, you camped and slept in a tent swallowed up by mystery. Your inflatable canoe almost went down but your then calm kicked in. You made it to shore, the night was chilly and the animals bold by your sleeping body.

I collect tree-ghosts to distract myself.

Maybe my books will consume me and it will be a pleasant death.

Meanwhile I have to sign my name here, here and here. As if I got time for that (nobody does).

In the soft blue morning you called your friends and made peace while I amended the love songs meant for you to include me, without you.

Old letters from Dad

The fibers in your expensive covers
that you use to hide yourself in, you see
and I see you are so nostalgic.
We are your daughters,
we rub your back we feel the weight
of your womanhood the weight of your
years spent invested. We are locked
in our own vein of this heavy
melancholy in our weeping
and I started it and I am
sorry and it is strange to let go
for the first time in months and just
let my body react.
The fibers in your voice that I use
to hide myself in, all those times
I laid in your lap and you ran your
fingers through my hair,
and my sister, her goddess legs
and brown eyes, now red, and we stay
there for a few moments, sinking.

Bethany Price graduated from the University of Wisconsin-Milwaukee in 2012. Her chapbook *All I Wanna Do* was published in the summer of 2013 through **Pitymilk Press**. Her hobbies include asking questions, reading fiction, staring up at where tree meets sky, and drinking caffeine. She works in a retail store and a jazz café.

www.ingramcontent.com/pod-product-compliance
Lightning Source LLC
Chambersburg PA
CBHW031209020426
42333CB00013B/859